BACKGROUND CHECK

HYBRID IMPACT FITNESS

1900 Cobb International Blvd NW,
Suite C,
Kennesaw, GA 30152

HYBRID FIT FOOD

3415 Old 41 Highway NW,
#700,
Kennesaw, GA 30144

BOOK ORDERS AND ONLINE COURSES

www.backgroundcheckthebook.com

BACKGROUND CHECK

7 KEYS TO UNLOCKING SUCCESS IN LIFE AND BUSINESS

GREG MCNEAL
GREG POINTDUJOUR

with Visionary Writing

Level X Publishing

Background Check
© 2019 Hybrid Impact Fitness

This edition: ISBN: 9781704110417

Published by: Level X Publishing (in association with Amazon Publishing)
Cover Design by: Natalie Brown
Cover Photo by: Tangie Renee Photography
Interior Design by: Visionary Writing
Editing by: Visionary Writing, Tyhi Conley, De'ja Wilcher, Alyssa Priya Hall, Christian J. Brown, Dionne Latham

First printing November 2019 / Printed in the United States of America

Dedication

"As a man thinketh so is he!"
This book is dedicated to everyone out there who has ever dreamed and aspired to be great. To those who dared to step out on faith despite being stereotyped because of a particular race, gender or environment. To my seven children Taviee, Aurmonie, Armarion, Amari, Shakia, Ardavion and Nevaeh. You are the reason I get up daily and work so hard so that you don't have to. To my beautiful parents George and Sharon for birthing me and instilling values within me that wouldn't allow me to compromise righteousness under any circumstances. Dad you taught me how to be a man.

To my siblings Cherone, Tressie, Myka, Kiya, Randy, Anton, Tavarra, Tamara, Roderic, and Marcus. You guys constantly pushed and motivated me to want better for myself and for US. To the Matriarch Rosemary McNeal for just holding the entire family together at all cost. To the Patriarch William Means who was my everything, continue to rest on. Thank you to the host of Aunts, Uncles, Cousins and friends who've supported me from the beginning and always encouraged me to be the BEST! Last but not least. This dedication is also for any individual who has been convicted of a crime, trying to reenter society from a place of incarceration. I hope this book will give you the keys and the driving force behind being your OWN BOSS. THIS IS FOR THE STREETS!!

Greg McNeal

To my family, friends, future unborn seed, and to the future generation of entrepreneurs, inventors and great thinkers that our book and story will inspire. To anyone that receives motivation to be their greatest self. This is a true reminder that no matter your situation or circumstance, you can always find a way to overcome it with the right mindset, humility, faith, environment, growing pains, purpose, and use of the free game we gave you in this book. The world will be yours.

Greg Pointdujour

Dedication

We'd both like to give a special dedication, and thanks to Elijah
Weems - who at the young age of 23 ,re- energized us at a time
where we seemed to be content or rather complacent. Sadly, he lost
his life to a senseless act of gun violence - but his legacy, his vision,
his passion, his smile and all that have been inspired by him will
continue to be inspired through US!! Rest up lil bro.

Greg McNeal
Greg Pointdujour

FOREWORD BY VISIONARY WRITING

This partnership with Money and GP started at a Commerce Club meeting in Kennesaw, Georgia. I gave a brief introductory speech telling my name and giving a spiel about my company. I was easily the youngest one in the room, but I felt more motivated than intimidated. After the meeting, I met Greg McNeal and he told me that people have always told him that he needs to write a book because he has an interesting story. My idea of interesting was definitely not a story that included a basketball player who was my age making enough money to feed his city. However, when he fully explained his journey, I knew that we had crossed paths for a reason.

After visiting the gym and meeting GP, the story began to evolve even more. I thought to myself, "This is crazy. There's no way that two brothas with the same name and similar backgrounds end up as business partners. God had to have designed this." After working through this project with GP and Money, my initial thought was confirmed. The desire that these guys have to give back to their community is beyond inspiring. As an African-American college student in Kennesaw, Georgia, I'm aware of the blatant lack of positive influences that look like me.

Foreword by Visionary Writing

The more time I spent with the Gregs - the more I learned and was truly inspired. I met with them in their 6,000 square foot training facility, then ate at their Café', Hybrid Fit Food. They made me believe anything was possible with proper preparation and relentless dedication. The endless knowledge that I was able to absorb Is helping me build my own business. It reminds me of a Jay Z quote that I've heard Money say multiple times, "No, Hov did that so hopefully you won't have to go through that." Greg P and Greg M laid it all out on the table in this book. They give a blueprint of how to unlock the power inside of every human being and reach the level of success that you're seeking. They have the keys, and they're giving them out in this project.

THE 7 KEYS

"If you want to go fast, go alone. If you want to go far, go together."

-African Proverb

HUSTLER'S MENTALITY

I

Where It All Began

Where It All Began

While I may have lacked proper resources, the entrepreneurial mindset was embedded in me as a kid. My name is Greg McNeal A.K.A Money. Growing up, I would sell almost anything I could get my hands on. My grandfather Jesse started me off as a young entrepreneur by teaching me how to sell Icee cups. I sold them to the children in my Westside neighborhood. At nine-years-old I was charging friends to play my Nintendo. I would also sell the fortune cookies my dad brought home from his job. I constantly pursued new ventures. Eventually, the hood began to call me Money.

As I matured, the inner-city environment began to take its toll. Violence and drug use was prevalent throughout the community. My parents eventually became users.

A functioning, peaceful household, quickly transformed into what could only be described as a crack house. Even with all of this going on my entrepreneurial niche ceased to change. Without a positive outlet for my talent I went from selling icy cups to friends, to selling drugs knee-deep in the streets of Chicago. What a difference 10 years made.

I studied my environment, and the dealers before me. What I learned was that I needed a clean brand to execute my entrepreneurial vision. I placed an emphasis on avoiding violence and making sure my team was good. If anyone got locked up I was there with bond money immediately to build a sense of trust and loyalty. In the meantime I was helping my community with my ill-gotten gains. By twenty-one, I was supplying over eighty percent of the Westside of Chicago directly or indirectly, and by then I had counted my first million dollars.

More Money, More Problems

When the time came for me to expand my business, I proceeded to touch bases in all areas, same as I did with my childhood hustles. Beauty salons, restaurants, construction companies, gyms, I owned them all. In terms of impact, my lifestyle had proved fruitful, but ultimately, it couldn't be sustained. At the age of twenty-five, I received a 25 year federal prison sentence for conspiracy to distribute cocaine and a five-year consecutive sentence for a gun charge in furtherance of the crime.

A key attribute in a humble individual is self-awareness. In prison, with nothing but time to reflect on my actions, I learned that lesson. I came to the awareness that while I took care of many people; it came at a higher cost -- I halted the growth of others. The more money I accumulated, the more I assisted in creating households like my own. In the end, I admitted to myself that the bad deeds outweighed the good.

After nearly five years of fighting my case while in prison, I was released due to the 4th amendment illegal search and seizure violation. I acknowledged my wrongs and was subsequently given a second chance. To me, the process seemed like fate. Out of prison, I vowed that I would dedicate my entire being to helping others. To find and fulfill my destiny, I decided to leave Chicago. Only months out of federal prison, I moved to Atlanta, in hopes of bettering my life and building a solid foundation for my family.

Immediately prospering in a new city seemed unrealistic for a person with no corporate job experience, a conviction and no connections. I completely changed my perspective on life, a man who once counted over a million dollars cash was willing to work at McDonald's for minimum wage, if necessary.

During my prison stint, I developed a passion for
fitness, and because of that, I aimed for LA Fitness to
be my first legit gig. This is where I met Greg P. He
managed an LA Fitness in Kennesaw, Georgia for
three years, and eventually hired me. The chances of
two strangers having a similar background, a similar
vision, and the same name were slim, but it instantly
allowed GP and I to connect.I worked at LA Fitness
for all of two weeks. My final straw came at the end
of a 70-hour work week, where I received a $400
check.

The short change persuaded me to take matters into
my own hands once again. However, this time, it
would be legal. The humble pie that was served led
us to partner up, and take the next step in birthing
Hybrid Impact Fitness.

CHAPTER TASKS

- Where are you currently?

1. Write down your top 3 strengths or things you feel are natural gifts.

2. Write down two different ways you can generate income from each of your strengths/gifts.

CHAPTER JOURNAL

WRITE DOWN YOUR THOUGHTS

"Greatness festers in isolation and frustration." – TD Jakes

HUMILITY

2

There's No Secret Code

Humility

Humble people are often misunderstood, mistaken for the weak or insecure. But humility takes the utmost strength. Amid success it can be easy for your foundation to crack if not built properly in the beginning. We should allow our greatness to speak for itself, but it can be difficult in a society that encourages competition and rewards popularity. As a result of that the real difficulty lies in being modest. Humility is more than a key to prosperity. It's what separates those who are merely successful, from those who are spiritually fulfilled.

There's No Secret Code

True humility for us didn't show until we hit the lowest moments of our lives. Being humble can be learned from different experiences. For some, it can be a person or a memory that keeps them leveled. For others, it's their environment. Every tall castle once began with a single block. Don't look down on your small beginnings. We have been working together for nine years and can see the fruits of our labor. Looking back, however, we realize that it didn't start that way.

CHAPTER TASKS

- Define Humility

1. Write down the most humbling experience of your life?

2. What lesson did you learn from this experience that you feel can help you be successful in the future?

3. What are things you can do to remain humble as you move forward?

CHAPTER JOURNAL

WRITE DOWN YOUR THOUGHTS

"Greatness festers in isolation and frustration." - TD Jakes

EMBRACING
ENVIRONMENT
3

Overcoming Obstacles

34

Embracing Environment

My name is Greg P. long before I co-founded Hybrid Impact Fitness, I was a kid growing up in Irvington, N.J., whose parents arrived from Haiti with nothing more than a middle school education.Never be ashamed of where you come from. It's a universal concept, one meant for those raised like us, in the inner city, trying to escape the negativity they've seen as well as those born with a fortune, but want to prove that they've earned what they've achieved, and all those in between. Even if it's indirectly, the environment you're raised in will surely affect you as a person. The challenge is finding that bright spot in the journey then proceeding to shine it on others.

To put the situation in perspective, in 2019 the FBI reported that Irvington's crime rate was higher than 92% of the state's other cities and towns. I grew up in America's crack epidemic in the 1980s. The city's image was no better but worse.

The Danger

Each day was more dangerous than the last. My parents worked tirelessly to provide for their three sons, all while making just over $3.00 an hour. As one can imagine, there were tough times. Still, those times molded me to become the man I am today. They shaped my life views, and gifted me with the mindset that I now carry daily.A part of that mindset stems from hearing the statistics like those previously mentioned and then going home to live the situation. In my eyes, the people in the community were to be cherished, not branded as criminals.

Like Father, Like Son

Living in the conditions of police brutality, racial profiling, gentrification, block shoot outs, lack of resources, and other disadvantages – it's only something you'd understand if you experienced it. The outside world attempts to look inside inner-city homes, but they could never paint the picture as accurately as I can. Primarily because those outsiders are often looking for opportunities to take over our areas and construct a new environment that puts money in their pockets. If these people looked a little closer, with a little more empathy, then they'd see people like my father.

Once my father adjusted to the lifestyle in the states, he found ways to earn extra money. His first move was to get his CDL license to become a truck driver. My father took his savings and purchased used cars, refrigerators, and other miscellaneous items for low prices and sold them for a profit in Haiti. My pops was an entrepreneur and an aid to his homeland.

Like Father, Like Son

Like many young men, I admired my father. Therefore, by watching him, I knew what to do with my own life: to become a businessman. Consequently, I've spent my life striving to reach my goal.

I took my dreams to college, where I graduated with a bachelor's degree in business management. The college experience afforded me the opportunity to gain an education and network with people from all different walks of life.

Bright Spot

Originally, I went to Dean College in Franklin, Massachusetts, where I played football. After suffering through an injury for two years in Junior College, I transferred to Jacksonville State University in Alabama. My injury subsequently caused me to lose sight of the vision that got me there. Like Greg M., I started to use my business mind unlawfully.

Traditionally, the South's gun laws are more lenient than in the North, also making them more accessible. I discovered a weakness in the system and began to traffic guns up north. I eventually got caught, leading to my arrest and subsequent conviction for conspiracy to sell firearms without a license and was sentenced to 18 months in federal prison. Even so, my mistake taught me my toughest, most vital lesson. I learned that it's okay to remove yourself from an environment that's no longer meant for you. That didn't mean that I was ashamed of New Jersey, it will always be my home. But it had taught me everything I could gain, and it was time to take the next step in my life.

Bright Spot

I realized I must leave home to create the life I desired. Still, instead of looking at my community through a negative lens, I chose to embrace my environment seeing it as the groundwork for life as an entrepreneur.

CHAPTER TASKS

- ## Describe Your Current Environment

1. Breaking the cycle, how can you use your environment to your advantage (outside the home & inside the home)?

2. Find somebody you think is doing life the right way. Write down how you can model their behavior.

3. What are three positive things you've learned from your environment you feel can help you to be successful in life and business.

4. What are three way you can help improve your environment whether it's your work place, community, household etc.

CHAPTER JOURNAL

WRITE DOWN YOUR THOUGHTS

"We need something that scares us, your greatest miracle will be in your scared place." –
TD Jakes

FAITH

4

Infiltrate, Educate, Vacate

Success is rarely an overnight venture. However, we must remain steadfast in our faith that we will bring our personal visions to life. This vision for us is the foundation for our journey. Everything that exists concretely before *us* began as an abstract thought. One thought leads to an array of thoughts, which complement each other so perfectly, that we now have created a vision for ourselves. There will be many who will not be able to grasp or relate to your vision because it is specific to you, as this vision was placed upon your head and heart to guide your personal path.

Infiltration is the First Step

The first barrier that must be broken is that of infiltration into your chosen industry or field. This is also the beginning of the test of your faith and level of desire for your goal because when we think of entering into something, we can often find ourselves thinking of what we lack compared to others who have been within this specific industry for a while.

However, this should not be the focus. Beginning the journey is the first step to conceptualize your vision, and we all have to assume our starting positions before commencing the race to our destinations. Fitness, health, and lifestyle were driving forces in our visions. In our pursuit for purpose, we both were lead to infiltrate a major gym which, in turn, helped us build our foundation within the fitness industry. It is not about how or where you start but rather that you take the initiative at all.

We infiltrated the same company at different levels, but that did not affect our visions. I happened to be a manager within the company during the time Money wanted an opportunity to gain employment. We had the same name and similar background. We also had a vast amount of understanding for the mental, emotional, and physical trials of those who become products of their environments. It seemed this moment was destined to intertwine our paths and to give us both a chance to enter and build our foundations. We had to go deeper than the face value of what lead us to our interest in fitness. Once we were both given the chance to be a part of a major gym, we were able to learn the backend. There we educated ourselves about aspects of what it takes to own a successful fitness company by working for a successful fitness company.

Education is Key

Knowledge helps to build and fuel the passion for your purpose. Working in your desired field gives you an opportunity to soak up vital information and gain resources. You will notice several different aspects that will prove to be beneficial to the value of your company. Take what you need and apply it. Use this opportunity as a stepping stone. As you move higher up the ladder of success each step will represent an obstacle you have overcome. During this time, you must maintain your faith.

The biggest reward of your starting position is the knowledge that can be attained. Observe your competition. Observe those rooting for you. Observe and assess what can be fixed and what cannot. Make this starting position beneficial by preparing for your next move. Learn from those who have come before you, so you can personalize your next move and make it the best for you.

The monetary gain may not be great at first, this is why sacrificing monetarily for the mental gain is a fair trade. The knowledge will provide more long-term overflow. Educating yourself about the system is important, but it is also important to study those who are a part of the system. Moving forward you should know what kind of people you will need to assist in building a strong system.

Enter the Water

When it is time to take action, things become real. This is when the saying "step out on faith" applies. Ask yourself. How strong is your faith? How confident are you about your purpose and path? How driven are you along this path? You may have gained entry into your desired industry, and you have managed to gain knowledge regarding the internal structure of the system. Money knew he was ready to pursue his path in the fitness industry because he observed those around him who were in the same field. He knew me, the perfect individual to partner with on this journey. We learned that **having a vision and no drive will only be a waste of your potential.** The timing is key. The resistance will be there, but you must be ready to leap.

Once we found a location, it took us a short time span of three weeks to sign our first lease. It was exciting. We prepared for so long. There was no resistance or hesitation. Everything flowed. It was clearly meant to be because of how soon things fell into place. With faith as our foundation, there was nothing that could stop us from dream chasing and putting our stamp on the fitness industry.

CHAPTER TASKS

- ## Visualize Your Escape

1. Write down the professional field that you desire to be in if not already in it full time.

2. Write down 5 companies that you would like to work for or with within the industry.

3. Write down 5 key things you want to learn from companies.

4. Write down your desired exit strategy.

CHAPTER JOURNAL

WRITE DOWN YOUR THOUGHTS

"Build a machine to reach your dreams, that's what a business is - a machine designed to help you reach your dream." - **TD Jakes**

_____
_____
_____
_____
_____
_____
_____
_____
_____
_____
_____
_____
_____
_____
_____
_____
_____
_____
_____
_____
_____
_____
_____
_____
_____

GROWING PROCESS

5

Execution

Growing Pains

One of the prominent inspirations for this book came from the Bureau of Labor Statistics study that we read. They reported that found that 24% of American businesses failed in the first year, and 48% didn't make it past the second year. Though the statistic is alarming, I'm sure lack of preparation was the main factor. screams "lack of preparation".

An Entrepreneur Must Be a Visionary

The most common mistake for a young entrepreneur when starting a business is underestimating your responsibilities. Far too often, young entrepreneur let their enthusiasm transition into impatience, causing them to skip steps. Those skipped steps lead to losses and hardships follow. Veteran entrepreneurs also face adversity, but the difference is in the response. An experienced entrepreneur is confident in their ability to adapt. The inexperienced tend to fold under the pressure. To build a long-running business one must look past the dreamy, glamorous outcome, and focus on the day-to-day tasks that will keep the business afloat.

"SLEEP IS FOR BILLIONAIRES."

The first factor in building a long-standing business is having a vision. While working together at LA Fitness, our vision is something we constantly discussed. We both had ownership experience prior to meeting, and we met while seeking knowledge for the industry we wanted to enter. We were trained to go, so it didn't take a series of sessions to create our brand. In fact, it only took *one*. The meeting took place during GP's lunch break and only lasted a little over an hour. We knew then we had something special. GP recently touched down from a mission trip to Haiti and was plotting on leaving LA Fitness. I was already gone and started to look for spaces. Before the lunch, we had no name, logo or business strategy. By the end, we procured all three.

To take the last leap of faith, we needed money. We had money saved - not enough to do everything we wanted, but enough to start. Along with the cash, we could leverage our credit to work in our favor. We decided to work in stages. First step was to secure a space, regroup, then attain everything else along the way.

Luckily, I found an opening, only a half-mile away from LA Fitness, and brought the idea back to GP. We met with the landlord and pitched the business. He loved it. The space hadn't been leased in over two years, so he was more willing to negotiate. Timing was great for the both of us.

There were two signing options: a five-year deal, and a three-year deal. In return for signing a five-year lease, he offered a build-out, and would finish the building until the space became functional for use. The cost of our unit, specifically, was $10,000. We expected to run our business longer than five years and the five-year lease came with perks. So to us it was a better deal. On the back end of the lease we'd pay our landlord back. It was perfect for both parties, we signed the lease in a week.

We used our own lines of credit for gym equipment and other necessities to avoid debt with investors or banks. We knew this was high-risk but had faith in the idea. If successful, the margin would explode. We were determined not to be back at rock bottom.

Our goal was to maintain one hundred percent of our business. We knew it would hurt if we lost with investors, but even more if we lost our own money. The decision not to use investors was the most vital in our execution. Since it was our own money, there wasn't a day we weren't totally invested. Each task, no matter how small they were, were to be completed to the best of our ability. We decided to do guerrilla marketing. We went door to door passing out flyers and networking. Whatever it took we did it. Our survival depended on it.

Put the Cherry on Top

Once your name is on a lease, responsibilities are immediately inherited. The month-to-month responsibilities included security deposit, rent, utilities, property insurance, billing, invoices and staff if you can afford it. Those responsibilities are to be handled before the owner pays himself. Taxes and permits must be paid as well. **It's crucial for the young entrepreneur to understand that, during tough times, there may not be a profit**. In these moments don't become discouraged. Don't allow fear to set in but keep the faith. By the time we opened our business, the only dominant social media platform was Facebook. We thought it was best that we go with a guerrilla marketing strategy. We suggest you try this even in the age of social media. Stepping outside and selling a product helps you get in touch with the community.

The entrepreneur is forced to share their story with individuals and begin to learn them as well. It was no different for us. We made a plan to attack those In our immediate proximity. We made flyers, class schedules, as well as hit the parks and small businesses to gain clientele. In addition to the flyers, we organized a Groupon promotion. The word began to spread, and we didn't hesitate to capitalize. We asked our clientele for a list of people they believed could potentially become clients. The referrals worked the best and quickly became half of our business clientele.

After seven months we outgrew our space. Our five-year lease agreement officially backfired, and we had to find a way out of it. Ironically, the property foreclosed, and we had no other choice but to move. We were blessed to secure a second, larger location. However, this presented a new set of challenges. It was twice the size of our first location, and our overhead had doubled.

This meant we needed to generate more income. We found ways to build interconnected businesses within our location. We started a meal prep service for our clients and the community, where they would come in and pick up their meals on a weekly basis. We also began selling hybrid apparel to generate more income and increase our brand awareness. Our second facility was in a prime location, centered between two high school. The location provided access to a large number of student athletes. Our plan and vision was to train them.

Although the meal prep was successful, it also provided challenges. It cut into our gym operations and we didn't have a staff to accompany the capacity of work that needed to be done. This led us to open Hybrid Fit Food, the first of several healthy eating restaurants.

Once again, there was a totally different set of challenges with the restaurant. As fitness directors and nutritionist, we weren't accustomed to dealing with food inventory, staffing, health code regulations, and more. So as serial entrepreneurs, we learned that new businesses mean new problems.

We learned that our daily challenges from business to business will constantly be changing, but the one thing that will never waver is our ability to write out a plan and execute it. We stayed in our second gym location for five years before moving into our third, and current, location.

The leasing process for our third gym location, as well as our cafe, was similar to how we captured the first - we found openings that weren't filled in at least two years, and the cycle continued. We didn't start with much, but the business is now the one we envisioned in the beginning. The slow start, the overhead fees, the insurance, the utilities, the security deposits, the marketing, the invoices, the taxes and the patience were all obstacles. Once the vision became tangible, we knew the work was worth it. The key is that any hardship should be overcome, not avoided or abandoned. So, for the young, hungry entrepreneur who's eager to get started, **keep the passion, but don't let it turn into tunnel vision.** Plan properly so you can be prepared, and don't let your mistakes kill your dream.

Once you have your foundation for your vision, the execution must begin and never stop. Although there are obstacles in business that cannot be accounted for or anticipated, planning and executing helps to keep your vision alive and give it breath. Planning gives your vision a sense of life because as you plan, you start to see the vision mentally before it becomes a physical manifestation. The more it feels real to you, the more excitement and drive you will have for your venture to become real. As mentioned, despite planning, there will still be situations which may appear to be methods of demise, but do not become discouraged. Most uncomfortable situations and positions are only preparing you for a much-needed change. Sometimes, in entrepreneurship, setbacks become pedestals to help us reach our goals in a smoother fashion.

Trust the process. Sometimes, our greatest blessings will be disguised as our greatest setbacks. In entrepreneurship, when a venture is meant for you, there will be little resistance. Our answer was practically handed to us when a legal battle ensued surrounding the space, and it was foreclosed on. We knew this was simply a pedestal to raise us to newer heights. We were then able to pursue a space that could contain our blessings and continue to help us flourish.

Continue planning and working hard. Your calling will make room for you.

CHAPTER TASKS

- How Will You Execute?

1. Write down your vision of where you want to be in life and business.

2. Write down 5 actions steps you can take immediately to get closer to the vision you wrote above.

3. Write down a timeline to execute your vision.

CHAPTER JOURNAL

WRITE DOWN YOUR THOUGHTS

"Instead of wondering when your next vacation is, maybe you should set up a life you don't need to escape from." - **Seth Godin**

PURPOSE

6

The Why

Greg McNeal
&
Greg Pointdujour

While we were in prison, we could've easily crumbled and given up. Through the course of our lives, we learned that in the darkest moments, there is still light at the end of the tunnel. There is still a purpose burning inside that screams, "*this is not the end, there is more to life, you have a purpose.*" There's a divine power writing the script of your life, even when it doesn't seem like it.

Are you aware of the beauty of a seed while it's buried beneath the dirt? As a seed begins to grow you can start to see its full potential. You have to search deep within and find what truly resonates with your spirit, because that is where passion is born. A purpose without passion is equivalent to faith without works. A purpose can provide direction, but passion will fuel your drive. Purpose will push you when your back is against the wall and you can't find a way out.

The Why

Your purpose can also be recognized as your "why." Which is really about the motivating factors deep down inside that drive us daily. For us, it's the people who look up to us for inspiration. It's our families that depend on us for security and assurance. It's our clients that depend on us to elevate their health *and wellbeing*. It's you, reading this book, looking to us for inspiration and guidance to unlock your success in life and business.

The Lightbulb

Self-reflection is a key starting point. You have to self-reflect to figure out where your gifts and talents are. What are you specifically good and gifted at? Use that as a stepping stone to build upon, when you feel lost, and uncertain. Remember your purpose. Feeling lost may trigger a mental eclipse, and you could lose yourself in the moment.

Remembering your purpose will give you some cushion to fall back on. Remember your gift and why you want to do it. Our gift is fitness, health, and overall wellness. That's our gift, and it comes easy to us. Even though we can do this in our sleep we still strive for greatness. Our purpose fueled by our drive is the right combination needed to inspire and motivate the masses. It comes to us so natural that it seems effortless.

I always knew my gift was in me. Through my college years while playing football, I always worked out in the gym. I would help others work out or make workout plans. Eventually I cracked the code and learned how to use my gift to build a career and make an impact. When I was locked up, a light bulb in my head went off. I knew then what I had to do. Stripped from my freedom, I went within focusing on my goals. I knew I'd be a personal trainer and use my gift to empower others.

Why You Shouldn't Doubt

I heavily respect Jay-Z and his rise to success. If Jay-Z didn't have belief in himself he would have never become a billionaire Mogul who started off as a rapper. He has a billion-dollar fortune which was reaped from everything he has sown. He planted *several* seeds that will benefit him and his family for a lifetime. Our background is similar to his. He probably didn't predict such a successful outcome, neither did we. When you have experienced the bottom, it humbles you and sets a clear example of where you don't want to be again.

To Serve

Simply put, purpose is having a reason. Personally, I believe my purpose on Earth is to serve. That's what brought GP and I to the path of health, fitness, and nutrition. We now attempt to save lives one day at a time. Finding your purpose will include what we've talked about throughout this book. You must have humility, faith, vision, goals, and a plan of execution.

These are all building blocks which can be used to construct a solid foundation. I would encourage using "the 7 P's" - **Proper Planning and Practice Prevents Piss Poor Performance**. If you are still questioning the definition of purpose at this point in the book, I want to make one *final* declaration. Every defining moment of your life will be determined by your mental state. If you're incapable of believing or having faith in yourself, you will never discover the true reason you were placed on Earth. This is why I believe that without the right mental space, *you will fail*. Get in the right mental state, become more organized, and start making small goals. They will train your mind to accept winning, and eventually you'll be prepared for the victory lap. Speaking of victory lap, we would like to pay respect to the late great Nipsey Hussle, who once said:

"SPOKE SOME THINGS INTO THE UNIVERSE AND THEY APPEARED. I SAY IT'S WORTH IT, I WON'T SAY IT'S FAIR - FIND YOUR PURPOSE OR YOU'RE WASTIN' AIR"

CHAPTER TASKS

- ## What's Your Purpose?

1. Identifying your why! It's the thing that wakes you up everyday, motivates, and inspires you.

2. Identify your purpose. It's the thing you were called to do with your life.

3. List how you can visualize your self-fulfilling your purpose.

CHAPTER JOURNAL

WRITE DOWN YOUR THOUGHTS

"You will never find your way in safety. You must confront your fears - this means failing, shortcomings, etc." - **TD Jakes**

FREE GAME

7

Knowledge is Power

Greg McNeal
&
Greg Pointdujour

Free Game

There's a famous saying that emerged from the hip-hop culture that goes "the game is to be sold not told." The phrase became so popular that even Snoop Dogg made it the title of his third studio album. While there's not a phrase for it in business, the concept is one that's silently followed. As businessmen, we can see how concealing information for a cost can be beneficial financially. However, as men whose life mission is also to help others, we'd like to deviate from that statement.

The Test

Along the bumpy journey to successful entrepreneurship, the principles, which we covered in the previous chapters, will be tested. When the time comes to making the tough decisions, you may have to choose between your morals or your business. Without proper guidance, a young entrepreneur will likely make the wrong decision. Enough of those wrong decisions and you have a person who will eventually abandon those principles for good. We believe there is a flaw in the philosophy. When information is kept from those who seek it in the end, it's the game itself that will suffer. In this final chapter, we'd like to oppose the norm by sharing the knowledge that could help make those decisions easier. We call it "free game".

Build a Strong Team

A strong team isn't necessarily measured by its numbers. You need quality people who are strong in different areas. When looking for the right team members, the first place a young entrepreneur should look at is themselves. Look for people who have some of your same qualities. The partners you choose should complement your strength by specializing in your weaknesses.

Gather

Once you've done the soul searching, the next step is actually gathering the team. This highlights the importance of networking. When searching the whereabouts of your future team will depend on your needs. For instance, are you looking for a temporary partnership or a permanent one? What is your end goal? Are you looking for someone that's willing to work towards that vision or someone who'll bring along their own? These are determining factors when deciding where to look, and who will make a good fit.

Strength in Numbers

Once you build a team , it's the leader's job to now examine the strengths and weaknesses of those members in order to put them in the best position to succeed. It should be expected for your team to be good at meeting deadlines, showing up on time, communicating, etc. A telling sign of an exceptional team member is one who takes the initiative. In a case where a team member is doing poorly up to the team leader to get them back on track. If you recognize the partnership with a team member isn't a good fit it's best to terminate them early. A troubled employee can become cancerous to the team. Don't risk all you have built.

Planning for the Worst

For a more seasoned entrepreneur, we would suggest applying for a key insurance policy. It's a life insurance policy specifically meant for a business partner in the event of an untimely death. There is no fixed amount a businessman should buy. Rather, the amount depends on the plans of the business incase of an untimely death. If you're a sole owner then the money may be used for the heir to pay off debts and close down the business. If you're ensuring a key partner or employee, then it could be used as a financial cushion to compensate that person's income. It could also be used to buy out the spouse of the deceased partner because the spouse would be entitled to 50% of the business in the event of a death. The entrepreneur should buy the necessary amount to execute their plan, whichever they may choose. The subject may be taboo. As much as a person may like the idea of living forever, it's obviously not a reality. To make your own decision on your legacy the conversation is necessary. Far too often, the business owner skips this process. The result of this mistake could likely lead to a closed or bought out business.

Reinvesting in Your Business

Once your business begins to flourish, and you've paid your debts, a portion of the profit should be used on reinvesting. The decision on how is up to you, depending on the type of business and its needs. We found that, for our business, reinvestments into equipment, marketing, interconnected businesses and education proved to be the most fruitful.

Interconnect

At some point in a successful entrepreneur's career, the possibility for growth will appear. When that time comes, look to start an interconnected business. This means to start a new business that may be related to your original. For example, to complement our gym, we created a herbal supplement line by the name of "Hybrid Fit Nutrition." We opened a cafe filled with healthy eating options and created the Realionaire Lifestyle Brand - which includes apparel, merchandise, a podcast, as well as a network of business professionals. The ability to intertwine all of these different businesses under one umbrella is what gives us the capability to call ourselves serial entrepreneurs.

Educate

Arguably the most important reinvestment is in education. No matter how long an entrepreneur has been in business, there's no way to know everything. Still that ignorance should be used as motivation to strive for perfection. Educate yourself by reading books, getting certifications or even going back to school. Furthering your education is needed to adapt to new social climates, and improve the services you have to offer.

Through our examples, the hope is for the growing entrepreneur to realize that reinvesting can be used on a minor expense, like light bulbs or a seating area, to major expenses like an employee. The point is to stay consistent, and always look to improve your business.

Educate Part Two

With this free game, we not only hope that the entrepreneur learns from these mistakes, but also from our actions of sharing game. When you start to view every decision through a competitive lens, like there's not enough success to share, that means the process is getting the best of you. If that moment comes, look back on the principals that got you to where you stand. Think about your story and where it's headed, and all the people that helped make it happen.

Only then will you be able to realize that your path shouldn't be affected by those you're comparing yourself to. It should only be affected by the people you intend to help. When the time comes for you to share your own story, take the game you were given, put your own twist to it, and help those who continue to think they must do it all on their own.

BOOK JOURNAL

Write Down Your Goals | Set Deadlines | Take Action | Get a Mentor

Name: _____

Made in the USA
Middletown, DE
28 December 2019